A Pocketful of Daisies

Copyright © 2020 Christine May

All rights reserved. No part of this book may be reproduced in any form or by any electronic or mechanical means, including information storage and retrieval systems, without permission in writing from the publisher, except by reviewers, who may quote brief passages in a review.

Published in 2020 by The Independent Publishing Network

ISBN: 978-1-83853-265-9

www.christinemay.com

Dedicated to the greatest love of my life, Emily Poppy born 11 May 2012

Introduction

This book is a celebration of a seven year long love story, so far, with my daughter. Over the years, I have collected the milestones and humorous happenings of her development.

Growing up happens so fast, I felt it was important to document what may otherwise be lost to memory.

May this book inspire you to capture your own child's precious moments or let the pages become a reflection on the magical process of becoming a person.

A Pocketful of Daisies

Christine May

0-6 months

0-6 months

The cherry tree was blossoming outside our flat the day you arrived.

0-6 months

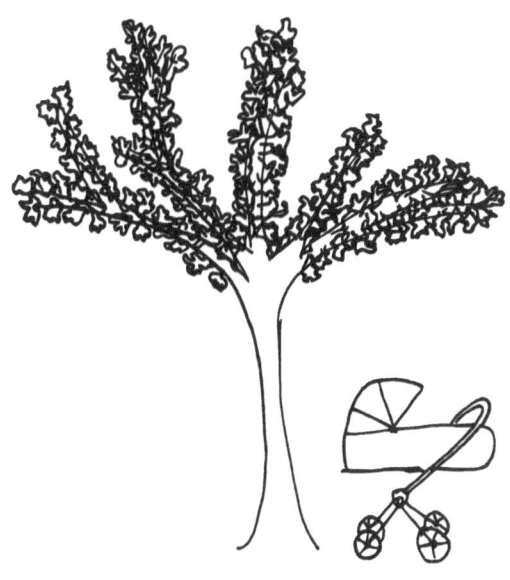

0-6 months

Your little fingers waving magically as if still in water.

0-6 months

0-6 months

I lie on watch, waiting to hear your next breath arrive.

0-6 months

0-6 months

I learn to negotiate the floor boards
so as not to wake you up.

0-6 months

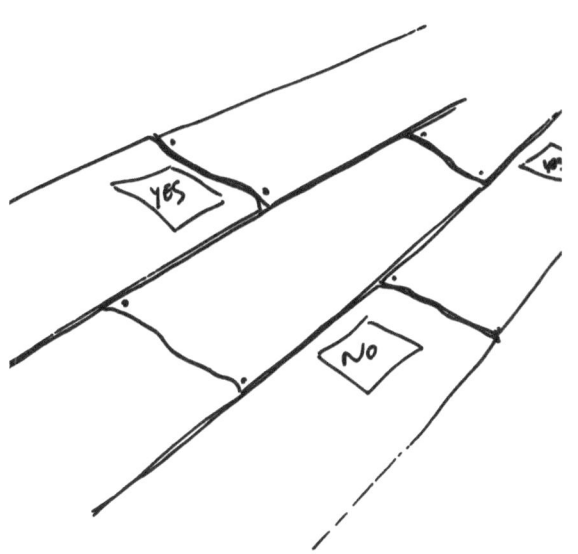

0-6 months

I walk the pram over the cobbled parts of the pavement, because bumpiness sends you to sleep.

0-6 months

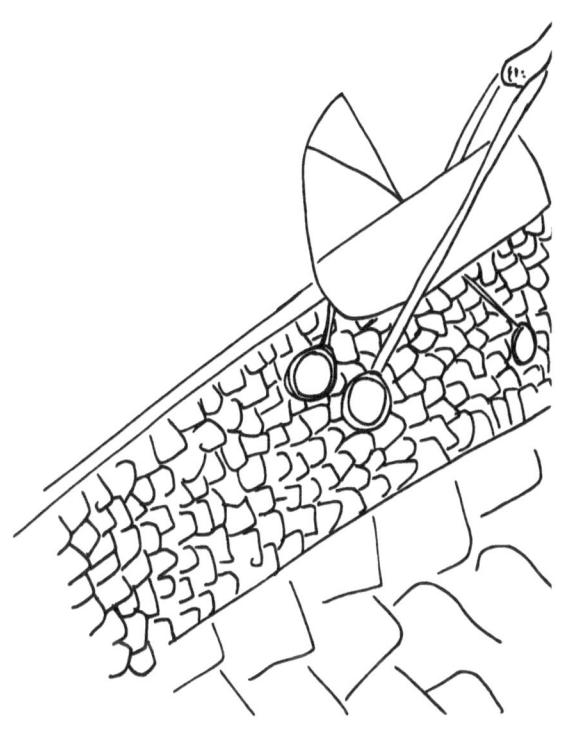

0-6 months

Eventually you fall asleep after I've rolled the pram 100 times over the door sill.

0-6 months

0-6 months

Your sudden hunger in public makes me hunt out private benches in graveyards to feed you.

0-6 months

0-6 months

Your smile reveals your full approval of bubble baths.

0-6 months

6-12 months

6-12 months

The kitchen walls show the remnants of your appetite for sweet potato puree.

6-12 months

6-12 months

One by one, your smile starts taking shape.

6-12 months

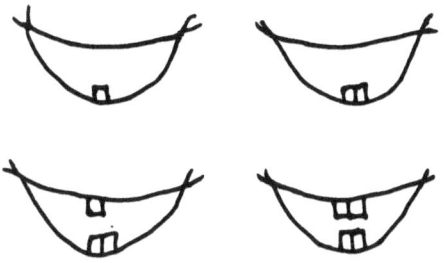

6-12 months

The realisation that love is:

Months of feedings
Years of nappy changing
A decade of tooth brushing

6-12 months

6-12 months

You drag yourself forward on your arms across the floor, just like a little soldier.

6-12 months

6-12 months

You learn to pull yourself up,
grabbing lipsticks off my
dressing table.

6-12 months

1 year

1 year

You're running on the summer grass picking daisies, putting them in your pocket.

1 year

1 year

One of your first words is the name of your eternal friend since birth: Wabbit

1 year

1 year

You throw a tantrum at the boarding gate because you can't get onto the aeroplane fast enough.

1 year

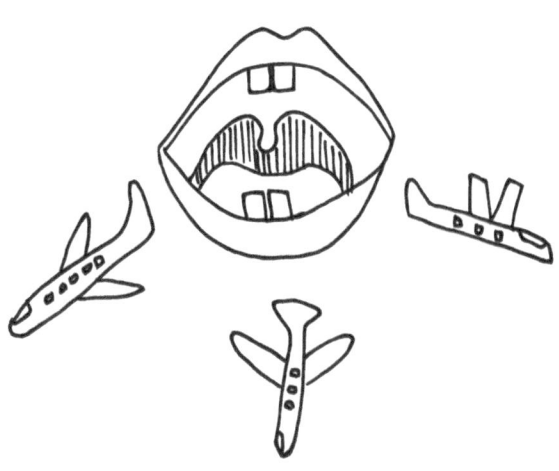

1 year

You cry all the flight because you couldn't pick the seat you wanted.

1 year

1 year

You learn how to flip open the lid of our strawberry-flavoured Vitamin D and help yourself to a handful when I'm not watching.

1 year

2 years

2 years

When one of your soft toys is missing:

"Does Penguin go to daycare?"

2 years

2 years

There's no greater joy than putting a sleeping child to bed.

2 years

2 years

You insist on taking your dress off in a department store and run free with your nappy.

2 years

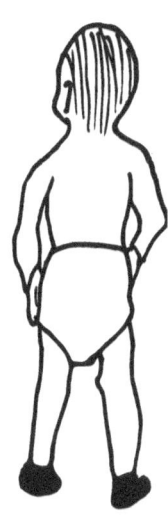

3 years

3 years

Love is baking a rainbow cake.

3 years

3 years

You go to bed with the frying pan and pink fridge from your doll's house.

3 years

3 years

I wake up to the sudden unfolding of your new pink and purple umbrella.

3 years

3 years

Helping out with the laundry is a dance when you can wear your "laundry ballerinas".

3 years

3 years

When the pee doesn't come:

"Mummy, I think the pee is asleep."

3 years

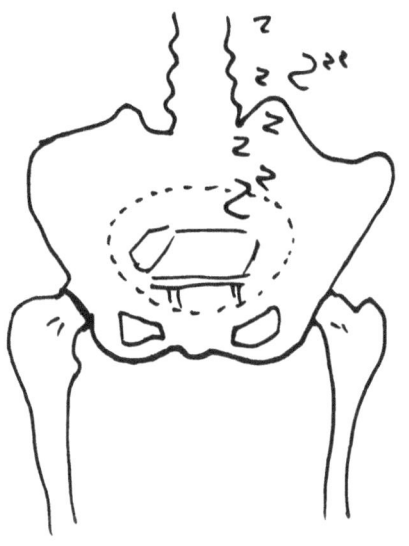

3 years

We invent the "lollipoop" as the reward if you go on the toilet.

3 years

3 years

The day you stop with your dummies, we hang them in the dummy-tree and you get a bike as a reward.

3 years

4 years

4 years

On a windy day:

"Look Mummy, the leaves are waving!"

4 years

4 years

"Mummy, can a mammoth eat a T-Rex?"

4 years

4 years

"Dolly has fleas in her hair."

"But that can't be nice."

"It's pleasant."

"Are they jumping?"

"Yes, they're skipping rope."

4 years

4 years

Love is mixing plaster for your Peter Rabbit cast, before making breakfast.

4 years

5 years

5 years

The result of loving your first atlas:

"Look Mummy, the puddle looks like the United Kingdom."

5 years

5 years

And when you can't sleep:

"Mummy, there are no real monsters, are there?"

"No, they only exist in your imagination."

"In books."

"Yes, exactly."

5 years

5 years

When getting farewell sweets is worth telling your friends at daycare it's your last day...when it isn't.

5 years

5 years

When you get your globe and understand time zones, it all becomes clear how Father Christmas manages to deliver presents around the world.

5 years

5 years

There is always a seat reserved in mummy's lap.

5 years

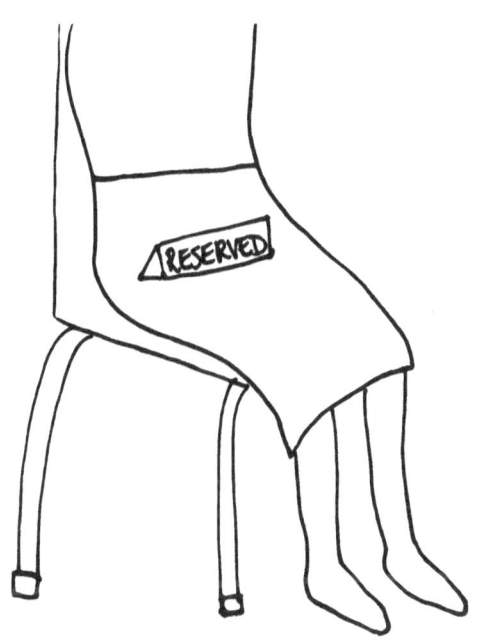

6 years

6 years

Your journey of voicing letters is the beginning of your love for books.

6 years

6 years

When you help with the laundry and all the socks are paired, you fold the left-over socks into an octopus.

6 years

6 years

When talking about accepting the offer of another school and if you have any questions about it:

"Do they also have a fruit break?"

6 years

6 years

I introduce the idea of the dream train that departs at your bedtime. You say you've got a ticket for a later train.

6 years

7 years

7 years

When doing your ponytail:

"I don't want it to stick out like little sharks."

7 years

7 years

On dropping your first corner tooth:

"Does the Tooth Fairy exist, or is it you giving the money?"

"When I was little, she existed."

"But was grandma putting the coins?"

"I don't know."

"My friend says that the Tooth Fairy and Father Christmas don't exist."

"What do you think?"

"I don't know."

7 years

7 years

After the Tooth Fairy has been in the night:

"Look Mummy! The bubbles on the money. And it looks like she's given a foreign coin."

You take out the money and count to £2.60. Plus there's a 2 euro coin.

"A special coin. It must be because the corner tooth was a special tooth."

7 years

7 years

Mummy's tooth brushing route

7 years

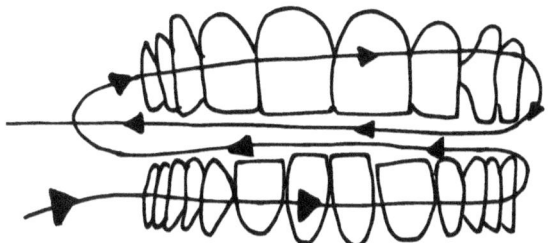

7 years

"Mummy, can you change who you love?"

7 years

Acknowledgement

This book would not have been possible without the unwavering support, dedication and patience of Luís Porém. You have my deepest gratitude.

www.ingramcontent.com/pod-product-compliance
Lightning Source LLC
LaVergne TN
LVHW041643060526
838200LV00040B/1696